TORI AMOS

IMAGES & INSIGHTS

PHOTOGRAPHY CREDITS:

Michael Friel: pgs 90, 91

Melody McDaniel: pg 94

Cindy Palmano: Front and back covers, pgs 1, 5, 10, 11, 12, 13, 16, 17, 18, 19, 22, 23, 26, 27, 32, 33, 36, 37, 44, 48, 49, 50, 54, 56, 57, 60, 61, 65, 68, 69, 70, 71, 81, 84, 85, 87, & 96

Rankin: pgs 3, 6, 7, 8, 9, 14, 15, 20, 21, 24, 25, 28, 29, 30, 34, 35, 38, 40, 41, 42, 43, 45, 46, 47, 52, 53, 55, 58, 59, 63, 66, 72, 73, 75, 76, 77, 78, 79, 82, 83, 88, 89, 92 & 93

Copyright © 1996 Omnibus Press
(A Division of Book Sales Limited)

Compiled by Kalen Rogers
Book designed by Amy MacIntyre

US ISBN 0.8256.1567.4
UK ISBN 0.7119.6115.8
Order No. OP 47856

Exclusive Distributors:
Book Sales Limited
8/9 Frith Street, London W1V 5TZ England

Music Sales Corporation
257 Park Avenue South, New York, NY 10010 USA

Music Sales Pty. Limited
120 Rothschild Street, Rosebery, Sydney,
NSW 2018, Australia

Printed in the United States of America
by Vicks Lithograph & Printing

"She's an archetype for the modern soul."

"An artist whose unabashed individuality means she
is often suspected of knitting with only one needle."

"Wise, warm and wildly charismatic."

"She's a Grade A, Class One, Turbo-driven Fruitcake."

"Some songwriters wash their dirty linen in public.
Tori Amos dries hers there as well."

"She remains endearingly harebrained, keen to bewilder, reluctant
to compromise, often hard to stomach, yet periodically magnificent.
Just the way, it would seem, that nature intended."

"Everybody told me this
'girl on the piano' thing
was never going to work."

THE TIMES (LONDON), JANUARY 21, 1994

"I think that
people who can't
believe in
faeries aren't
worth knowing.
I just think
alternate realities

make you
a good writer.
If your work
is any more
than one
dimension,
you believe
in faeries."

"Disciplined is not what other musicians would necessarily call me; they might call me obsessed and relentless and really out of control."

"For many years, I shut down that place inside myself that needed to rage, cry, ask questions, and basically just express herself. I made a conscious choice when I put 'Me and a Gun' on the record not to stay a victim anymore."

R.A.I.N.N. (RAPE, ABUSE & INCEST NATIONAL NETWORK: 1-800-656-HOPE) FLYER 1994

"The reason I love to play Bösendorfers is because
I think their whole manufacturing process is trying
to keep them
as unmechanical
- as unfactoryized
- as possible,
so that the soul
of everybody
who touches
one or works
with it is in there."

"It would be sad if you had

to go through

a rape

to hear what I was

saying in

'Me and a Gun,'

and to have compassion

for that kind of 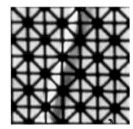 violation.

The strength that it takes

to get up and

sing that song

every night is

more than I ever

imagined."

"I don't know what a shrink would call me.

I don't want to know."

"Because Jesus maybe had
a sexual encounter
with a woman, did that make him less?

Was he soiled by it and
what does that say about women?"

"Who said that?
Who made up that rule?
And what grave is he in over in Europe?
Who cares?
The worms have eaten him.
It's over."
KEYBOARD MAGAZINE, SEPTEMBER 1992

"What girls do to each other is beyond description.
No Chinese torture comes close."
REALLY DEEP THOUGHTS FANZINE, WINTER 1994

"MOST PEOPLE WOULD RATHER BE SHEEP AND HAVE COMPANY

THAN STAND OUT ON THEIR OWN WITH ANTLERS ON."

"My songs to me, they really exist – I call them the 'babes.' They come with trousseaus or with a knapsack on their backs."
VOX, MAY 1996

"I'm a tomato freak, but sometimes you have to get it in ketchup form for people to be able to open to tomatoes."
BILLBOARD, FEBRUARY 17, 1996

"Say we didn't have bodies and blood and guts, but just released these little light energies like colors, then we could just merge. That's what making love is all about."
Q MAGAZINE, FEBRUARY 1992

"I realized I was still looking
to men for acknowledgment,
to make it OK. I was a vampire,
trying to take their energy,
to steal their fire."
THE LONDON OBSERVER, JANUARY 7, 1996

"Pianos are like people;
every piano has a
completely different
personality."
KEYBOARD REVIEW, FEBRUARY 1992

"Sometimes just because
it's a true statement
doesn't mean anybody
cares. So that's where
the skill of storytelling
comes in."
**UPSIDE DOWN: TORI AMOS FAN
CLUB MAGAZINE, ISSUE #6**

"The Ladies' Room is a secret society, and when those lipsticks come out it's the heaviest artillery in the world – the guys have no idea what they're in for."

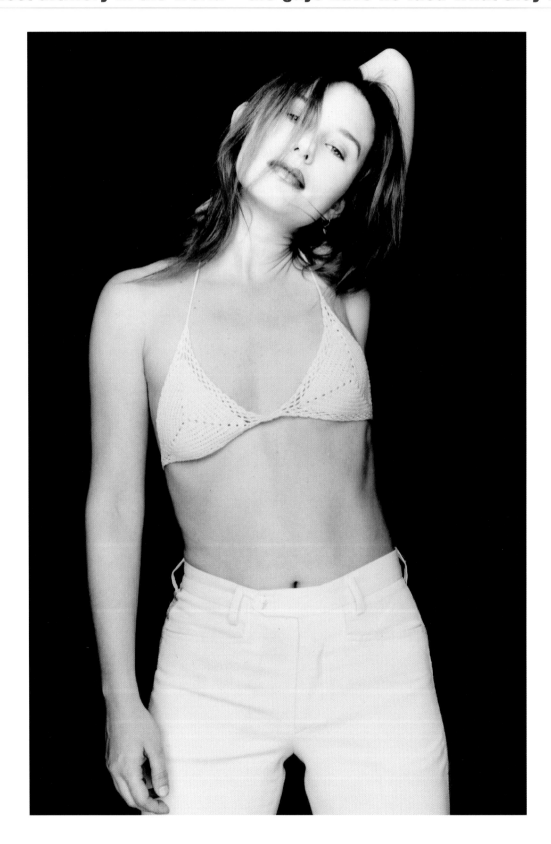

"Everything is secondary when the songs are coming. I don't know what kind of mother I would be; it would depend on how the songs felt about the baby. I'm a musician before I'm a woman, no question."

"I started finding the people inside me... the prostitute that's really angry because I judge her so harshly... the self-righteous virgin who knows everything about sex and has never made love."

GLAMOUR, AUGUST 1992

"Whether mankind or womankind has created what God has become, the point is it's a very strong force that has divided us within ourselves. I mean religion has divided the whole planet."

TAKE TO THE SKY
(UK FANZINE) WINTER 1994

"What gives it to you?
Does this rush, this being
in love, meeting someone
that has it, you want to be
close to it, you want to be
near them? No. You can
feed off them for a while,
but in the end, you're
just a vampire."

Z100 RADIO INTERVIEW, FEBRUARY 4, 1996

"I couldn't see that men's strength and physicality could be tender. I had to pretend I was a whore in my mind, thinking I was gonna get paid so that I could be detached and stay in control."
MELODY MAKER, FEBRUARY 1994

"I love speed. I love Formula One racing. I love the idea of travelling. Why do you have to leave your body to travel... why can't you go interdimensionally emotionally?"
Z100 RADIO INTERVIEW, FEBRUARY 4, 1996

"I'm the Queen of the Nerds."
VOX MAGAZINE, MAY 1994

"I do believe that music has a coding that nothing else has. That's why there are so many different styles of music. It's so exciting because so many people are carrying a similar message, but just a different vibration."
UPSIDE DOWN: TORI AMOS FAN CLUB MAGAZINE, ISSUE #7

"I think you're always striving for wholeness. I don't think you can put a time limit to it; it's really always another fragment coming your way as long as you're alive until you leave the planet."

"MY WORK IS MUCH RICHER THAN MY LIFE."

" I DON'T FALL IN LOVE MUCH. I MEAN, I FALL IN LOVE
EVERY FIVE SECONDS WITH SOMETHING BUT I DON'T GO
FROM BOY TO BOY. I GO FROM ARCHETYPE TO ARCHETYPE."

" So much happened to me in childhood and I still feel some kind of thread linking me with those days. I had times then when my spirit was broken. I remember when I was eleven and I thought my life was over."

MANCHESTER EVENING NEWS, DECEMBER 1991

"I'm too wacky for most weirdos. Who am I to judge?"

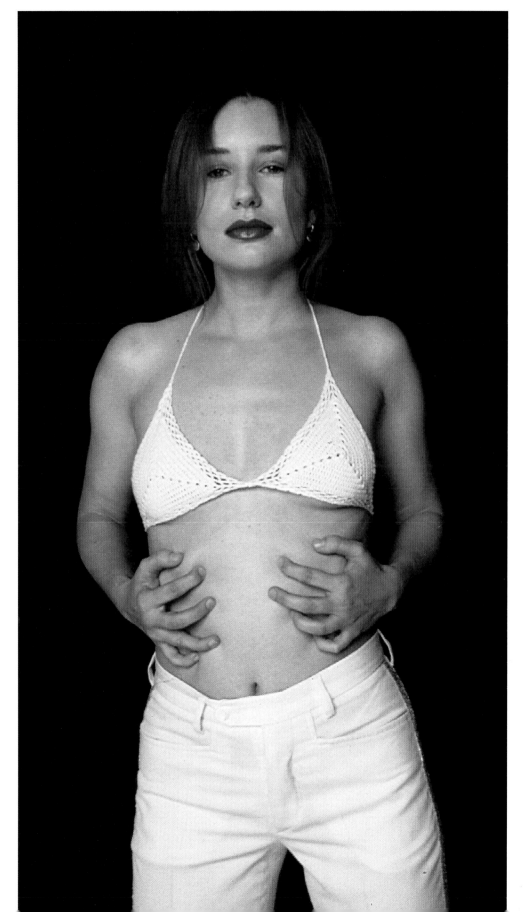

ENTERTAINMENT
WEEKLY,
JULY 12, 1996

"Since I was a little girl, I've been a musician first.
 I wasn't just an extension of the piano; I was the piano.
 That's how people looked at me."

"I'm a musician first, a food-lover second, a dirty mouth with feet, and a girl last time I checked."

"GO ON THEN,

ASK ME IF

I SLEPT MY WAY

TO THE TOP...

IN FIFTEEN YEARS

IN THE

MUSIC INDUSTRY

I HAVE TO TELL YOU

THAT NOBODY HAS

PROPOSITIONED ME.

NOBODY.

N O B O D Y ."

**"I'm not a part
of this business.
I was playing
music before
people were
peeing in
their beds."**

"I'VE GOT ENOUGH MONEY AT PRESENT TO FLY TO L.A. AND HAVE A GOOD

MEXICAN MEAL... AND THAT'S PLENTY."

"For all these years, I felt like all these different people at a dinner party.

When you've got the virgin and the whore sitting next to each other at dinner, they're likely to judge each other harshly."

"I DEFINITELY HAVE A WEAKNESS FOR SHOES.
JUST CALL ME THE IMELDA MARCOS OF ROCK 'N ROLL"

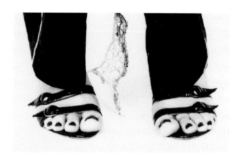

"A PIANO IS ALIVE BECAUSE OF ALL THE FEELINGS THE MEN WORKING ON IT PUT INTO IT."

PIANO AND KEYBOARD, MAY/JUNE 1996

"I THINK I'M METALLICA AND ASCAP DOESN'T ARGUE."

of
my
darkest
days,
Lucifer's the one who comes and gives me an ice cream."

SPIN, MARCH 1996

"Going to England on
my own was an
adventure. I was
trying to remember -
because I spent a lot
of lifetimes there
and I knew that -
I was just trying to
recapture parts of
myself, my power,
my memories."

"You can
compartmentalize
different sides
of yourself - put
them onto different
shelves and then
bring them out
when you
need them."

"You look at a crowded dinner table and you can see what's going on from what people are eating, the way they hold their forks, what they're saying and what they're not saying. Then you can look under the table and see what they're doing with their feet. It's the same thing with a song. It's creating an experience for someone to step into."
MELODY MAKER, NOVEMBER 1991

"I think that there is a lot of gushy mushy heart in my stuff, albeit it might be dripping with blood and mucus and maybe some chocolate, like our friend Elvis."

"It's like, the other guy may have peanut butter and jelly, but you're the one with the chocolate chip cookies. There's a balance there."

"I kind of feel I'm an archeologist when I'm making a record; I'm digging to discover things. I can't write something if I don't crawl in and sit behind your eyes and feel that."

"The music is the magic carpet
        that other things take naps on."

"I felt so intertwined with it that I had no identity except the girl at the piano. And I didn't respect it anymore, mainly because I wanted this piano to make me worth something. I wanted it to bring me friends and recognition... I was really using it the way you would use your last name or who your father was – or whatever you use to feel powerful."

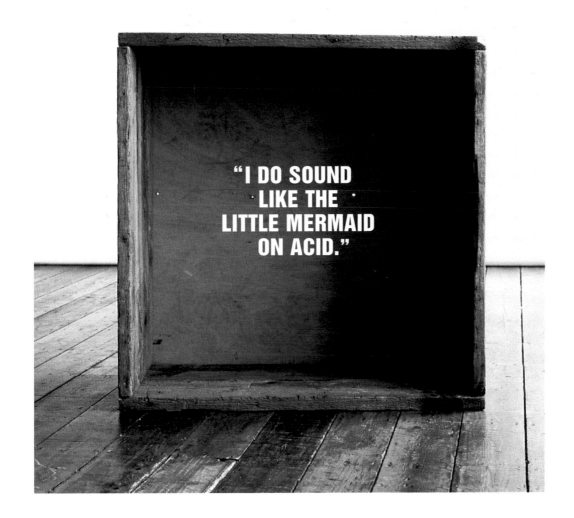

" The self is an endless vat of soup.

That minestrone does not stop.

You can change soups and the kettle keeps on boiling."

"Lipstick and lipgloss, always always.
I was in hospital recently and I had
my lipgloss in the operating theater."
Q MAGAZINE, MARCH 1996

"Really, I'm just translating. Once I accepted
that, that this isn't really about me, it's just
about tapping into different sides of Woman,
then I can take on these parts."
MUSICIAN, MAY 1996

"I usually get along best with the metal
guys... the real, real subversives.
I don't know, maybe it's because our
paths don't cross much, but I think
there's a passion there."
B-SIDE, APRIL/MAY 1994

"To take credit for them (the songs)
would be like taking credit for the
sunset if you're a painter."
ENTERTAINMENT WEEKLY, JULY 12, 1996

"Voodoo became something different once
the Christians came in. Before then, there
was an understanding of other worlds we
have chosen to disrespect."
VOX, MAY 1996

"All music is a pattern. I work
with different patterns and start
to push boundaries a little bit."
REALLY DEEP THOUGHTS FANZINE, SUMMER 1994

"I would like to think I'm a raisin girl, because in my mind they're more open-minded. Cornflake girls are totally self-centered, don't care about anything or anybody."

"When you have a woman coming out of a church, and she's yelling and expressing something, and she's screaming, you do not try to make that okay. You get in trouble when you try to trim the edges."

"You never can believe what you're up to when you're up to it of course."

"Playing is the only place where I've felt in touch
with my sexuality, my spirituality and my emotions,
and never, ever, ever anywhere else.
So my life is a bit tricky
because when I'm not playing,
I'm just trying to walk down the street."

"Feminism was an important shift that happened on the planet. But being a feminist isn't enough now. It's about being a whole person."

GEORGE, APRIL/MAY 1996

"Usually they sprinkle a few drops of water on your head; in my case they held my head under for thirteen fucking years."

NEW MUSICAL EXPRESS,
JANUARY 27, 1996

"The problem with my Christian upbringing was the role models for women. The idea passed down to you was that you couldn't be a passionate woman - not a virgin, but a woman – and still claim experience and wisdom."
DAZED AND CONFUSED MAGAZINE, FEBRUARY 1996

"When I was five, there was this Beatles album around the house, Sgt. Pepper's, and I was walking around with it, and my father said, 'What are you doing with that?' and I said, 'This is what I'm going to do.'"
Q MAGAZINE, FEBRUARY 1992

"Tape is a funny substance because besides sucking in sound, I think it registers everything that is happening within about a mile radius – the love that is made, friendships that are strained, caramelized onions..."
TORI PINK TOUR BOOK

"I don't hate men.
I give equal time in
my hate. It's acts of
people that I hate.
Whether they
be men or women,
it's their behavior
that I hate."

"I was a freak child
who had really
good rhythm. I'd be
invited to parties
simply because
I played the piano.
I quickly realized
that I had some
kind of calling."

" When I was very little
I got into big trouble
for wondering if Jesus
had a thing going with
Mary Magdalene."

THE GUARDIAN, NOVEMBER 1991

"The songs kind of stalk me, and when I just throw a line on them to try and get them out of my life they become pretty vicious. They come in. They move in, and they insist. Because they won't accept me lessening them, just because I'm uncomfortable."

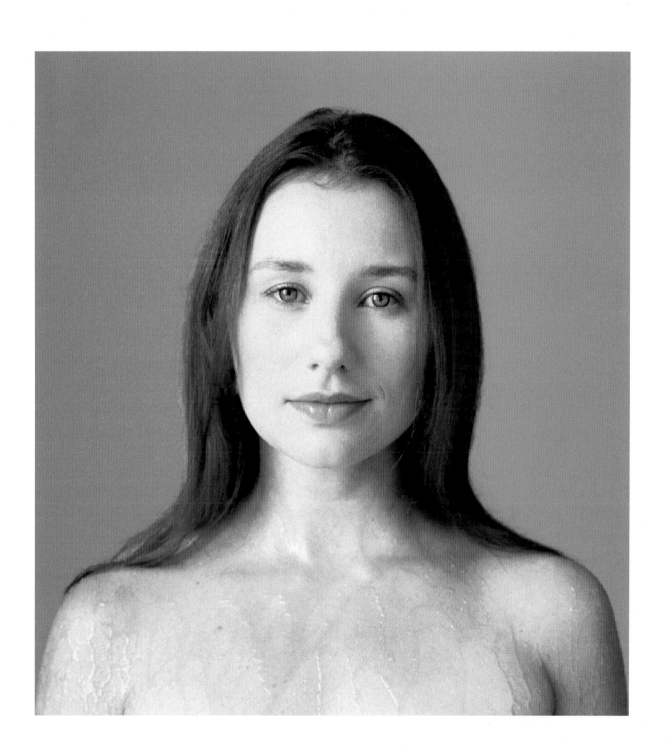

"Who wants some sniveling female all the time? After all, just because something happened to me and it was traumatic doesn't make it interesting. I have to get my scissors out and make sure I'm telling a story that works. It may be your own experience, but you can't be too precious."

" Truly, I was a sweetheart when I was little, like the Honeysuckle Fairy. Sweet. Sweet-pea. But Sweet-peas are not popular after second grade. Sweet-pea becomes Nerd really fast."

TIME OUT LONDON, JANUARY 22-29, 1992

"If I couldn't play, I've no idea what kind of bitter person I would've become. Because that's where I was able to express some kind of freedom without guilt. Guilt for passion."

"Cindy Palmano helped to put my vision out to the world, and without her it would've never been interpreted the way that it was and she has such a pure eye that she was able to go in there and capture my soul on film."

"I am garlic personified. Garlic and extra virgin olive oil. Garlic is garlic. You don't want it in ice cream, but you definitely want it when there are vampires around."

"Feminism is about the separation, not about the oneness. So I find the whole concept a bit stale. We need to get a bit futuristic here."

"If you buy into the fame trip, then you've really lost sight of why you're making music. Fame has just got to be a sideline. It goes with the territory, and once you understand that it's a bit like mosquitos. If you're going to live in the wilderness there's going to be mosquitos."

"The whole music industry is so much dictated by radio, and who are they dictated by? Advertisers. It's a vicious cycle. And where does it stop? When will musicians stand up and say, 'It's not about being lucky enough to get scraps off the table.'"

WOMEN TRY TO MAKE EACH OTHER CRAWL

SO THAT THEIR KNEES ARE BLEEDING."

"The most important thing to me
as a songwriter is the breath.
The most important thing I
could ever say to somebody is,
'Sometimes I just breathe you in.'"

"I'm not the kind of
woman who takes
things sitting down."